CONTENTS

W0013607

CHAPTER 1
THE LAND WHERE
EVERYONE IS OLD

Prepare yourself for a voyage of discovery. Immerse yourself in the knowledge of the wizened, the old and the dribbling senior citizen with gnarly hands. Experience the joy of the fading light, the ecstasy of extinguished hopes, the liberation of the grumpy old curmudgeon. Think of the words that a generation of baby boomers has all but forgotten how to use: geriatric, elderly, aged, wrinkled, lingering, ancient, old dear, old lady, old woman, old man, old guard, old stager, oldster, old timer, old world, old hat, old as the hills. Oldness is the natural human condition, yet is the state that dare not speak its name.

For many centuries, the great sages have been searching for a practical alternative to staying young. This is not easy in our modern lives, where the culture of youth is everywhere. Middle-aged men are buying motor bikes. Grandmothers are paying for cosmetic surgery to enhance their appearance. Pensioners believe that they are 'grey panthers'. Ageing rock stars are still wearing leopard skin underpants and dating the daughters of other ageing rock stars. Old people now prefer sex to cups of tea. The world is obsessed with staying young.

Defeating the tyranny of youth

But life does not have to proceed in this way. Deep within the cells of every being there is an inner cosmic knowledge that tells us that when we move beyond the self towards the eternal truth of time-bound life, in the jacuzzi of the soul we are all old gits. We must embrace our oldness. I am old. You are old. We are old. The Universe is old. God is older still. We must use the power of positive thought to enter the new paradigm where dementia is embraced and senility is seen as a welcome sign that the life force can't be bothered with you old fogeys anymore. You too can attain the state of ageing body, confused mind. Join me on the journey to the land where everyone is old.

Take a look at your body, but do not view it with the gaze of the time-blind person you used to be. Let your vision be enhanced by the knowledge of the new paradigm. Let the new awareness grow. Sometimes only the true seer of self-help publishing can ascertain the cosmic hand at work, urging your body on to mortal decay.

Why does your body appear to be so young? Is that natural? Is it good? Is this the way things are meant to be? The 45 or 50-year-old reader might feel the skin on their face and wonder why it appears to be so unnaturally smooth. Is there any reason your stomach should be taut instead of engulfed by elephantine folds of flesh? Why is your hair so unnaturally dark, when you should be using Grecian 2000? Isn't it time that just a little bit more cellulite was appearing on your thighs and you developed flabby ankles? Should you really be thinking about sex so much at your age? Why are you wearing a trendy jumper with a zipper and not a cardigan instead?

This never happened to previous generations. Once there was an easy transition from youth to middle-age to irritating senile old git with egg dribbling down your jersey. The more you peruse the symptoms of this apparently youthful body the more it becomes apparent that there is something deeply wrong at both the cellular and psychological levels. You have forgotten how to grow old.

Your body is failing to age because it has accepted the programming of the old paradigm. If you are to age successfully you must accept ten new assumptions. These are:

1. The world is objective; and you are objectionable

Some philosophers would have us believe that when we look at a chair there is no way of proving it exists. Human senses can deceive us, they claim. Perception can vary according to who is looking at the object and objective truths can change with scientific fashion. The best response to these opinions is to hit the philosopher over the head with the aforementioned chair and then ascertain if their view has changed.

To deny that there is an objective reality in which everyone ages is part of the conspiracy of the old paradigm. The oldness in our soul has been betrayed. Everyone, it seems, is ignoring the immutable laws of time and then attempting to recapture the essence of youth. Adults in their 50s and 60s are buying Harley Davidson motorbikes, jet-skis, Volkswagen camper vans and Hornby train sets. Yesterday's student radicals now believe that they can be rebels without a paunch.

The worst grey-haired nouveau adolescents speak of 'adrenaline rushes' and go rock climbing and skydiving. They speak openly of their second adolescence and believe that youth is wasted upon the young. They are learning how to use the Internet, logging on to Friends Reunited and having affairs with old schoolmates whom they last snogged when they were 15.

There is a collective denial of age in our society; only a few sages can see the objective reality. Beneath the tans built up in holiday homes or on delayed gap years, you are ageing at the sub-cellular level. Atoms, molecules, quantum bits, cells – they're all getting wrinkly. The Universe is ageing. The planet is ageing. You are ageing. Your body is part of the quantum soup and it is boiling over because you forgot to turn the hob off.

It can be most liberating to realise that you are getting old. Why bother to remember your bank card pin number when you can irritate bank cashiers and blame it on your deteriorating genes? Why rush in ticket queues when you can fumble for change and delay everyone standing behind you? Enjoy the frisson of standing up on buses way before the bus reaches your stop, swaying unsteadily and falling across the aisle every time the driver applies the brakes, and waiting for some fine-mannered young fool to offer you a steadying hand. The person who accepts their essential decrepitude ceases to care about losing everyday objects such as glasses cases, important letters and tax returns, and is instead at one with their scattered-mindedness. We must learn to touch our own frailty and then celebrate it. To forget and to bore is the beauty of our new world view.

2. Old people are the masters of Earth now

You will soon be in the majority. The number of octogenarians in Britain is set to treble in the next 50 years, from 2.5 million in 2002 to a whopping seven million in 2050. That's an awful lot of people to tut tut at young blokes in hoods hanging around bus shelters. Many of us are going to continue working past retirement age because governments can no longer afford our pensions. This presents limitless opportunities for the old codger in the office.

In the workplace, profound pleasure can be gained from the realisation that young people are all spoilt slackers. Because of their over-indulged childhoods, these youngsters expect the older workers to get everything done. Be baffled by the fact that young people completely fail to realise that work is punishment.

3. Mind, body and nasal hair are inseparable

Never underestimate the power of negative thought. All the evidence suggests that people who believe they are young continue to act as though they are young. To accept that you are getting old and will soon be paying for dentures rather than fillings requires an inversion of the old paradigm. The mind-body connection can be harnessed in the pursuit of oldness. In clinical tests, just the intention of growing old and giving up on modern music can produce drastic improvements in those inflicted with youth. Improving your mental attitude and the positive embracing of negativity can achieve very satisfying results in a relatively short period of time. Mental response becomes sluggish, balance declines, nasal hairs start to sprout and within days the patients are buying Burt Bacharach records.

4. We are all part of the quantum universe

Science can teach us nothing about the ageing process that we do not already sense at an intuitive level. Advances in quantum physics have revolutionized the way we look at age. Our bodies are masses of information and energy, while at the quantum level an active intelligence is urging every cell towards decrepitude. Those who eventually attain inactive mastery of the soul will at last rejoice in the advent of silver neck hairs.

Stars get old, collapse and form black holes where all matter is crushed to the size of a tennis ball and then we are whisked through the other side to a parallel universe, says Professor Steven Hawking. Although now he says that maybe he was wrong about the anti-matter universes and the theory of everything. Thus ruining several Star Trek plots. But what does he know? Like the rest of us he's getting old and even his Dalek voice box is in need of replacing.

DNA, which is the Lego brick of life, is urging us all to get on with snuffing it. That way our kids can carry on with their lives without having to ring Mum and Dad to say they arrived home safely after a weekend visit, or that yes, they have eaten three meals today.

5. Physicists have no dress sense – and you don't need to have one either

For the true sage, imbued with holistic wisdom, the greatest advance that physicists have bestowed upon humanity is the knowledge that dressing badly need be no bar to appearing regularly on Open University and the Discovery Channel. Beards, checked shirts, anoraks, novelty slippers, puffer jackets and stained lab coats are the badges of those who realise that bad taste is wasted upon the young. The true signifier of the old person is having the wisdom to give up on clothes. The old man who is at one with his inner curmudgeon is not afraid to wear sandals with white socks or brown corduroy trousers. The old woman who knows her state of decrepitude and accepts it will be happy to model baggy woolly tights and novelty aprons. Becoming old is to accept the glorious liberation of having absolutely no fashion sense whatsoever.

6. Be aware of awareness

Everything in our lives is conditioned by awareness. Every cell is aware of what you think about yourself. Feel the changes in your body at the sub-atomic level, experience the energy of age pulsing through your cells, the layers of skin dying and falling from your body every time you take a shower. Listen to your toenails growing. Be aware that your body is taking you on a spiritual sojourn towards eternity.

7. Bits of your body are falling apart every second

The atoms that comprise your body are millions of years old. Impulses of information pulse through your body telling you that you are knackered every nanosecond of the day. The body can only respond to the information we programme into it. If the information we send portrays youth as a positive life goal, then our cells become stuck in a pattern of regeneration. Thankfully, with negative thought and inner awareness, we can control this information surge through our bodies. In the new paradigm we must nourish our quantum flesh with the correct information: oldness is our ultimate goal, grumpiness the highest form of human attainment.

A 50-year-old on a delayed gap year has the same molecules as a 50-year-old who has given up searching for youth and made a dignified retreat to the vegetable allotment. In order to evade the prison of youth we have to feed the mind-body the correct core beliefs. Only when we nourish the body with the belief that we are old can we come to true acceptance of the ageing process.

8. We are all part of a fragmented cosmos

A breath taken in Grimsby is very different to one taken in Chelsea. One assimilates the scent of fish in the lungs, the other Chablis. Infinite energy fills quantum space; cars fill car parking spaces in nanoseconds. Energy is vibrating in fields, particularly fields in Wiltshire, when the locals get a little frisky after too much cider and then create crop circles. Your body is a manifestation of the quantum field. The world is in your body, your body is in the world. As the seers of Sister Sledge once revealed: 'We are family, I got all my sisters with me'. There is a unity between all things in the space-time continuum, from the macrocosm to the micro orgasm. The universe is a living mind. And it is telling you that you are going out of yours.

9. Time is absolute

Right from the Big Bang, God was setting his digital alarm clock. Just play the start of Pink Floyd's Time really loudly. As the Universe expands and the Sun threatens to go supernova, time is running out. It is in its running shoes and on its second marathon without even one of those silly silver foil blankets with a sponsor's logo on it to keep it warm. The field of time is flowing towards your demise.

To accept that life is bound by time is one of the most joyful discoveries the human mind can ever make. This enables the wise person to become a person driven by deadlines. Try telling a commissioning editor that time is a piece of boxed eternity. It certainly didn't work with this book. Time is rigid, trains always leave on time when you are late for them, and commissioning editors never accept even the most plausible of excuses for late delivery of copy.

10. We are all victims of ageing, dodderiness, feebleness and death
Humans have to age. It is as inevitable as storm drains backing up and flooding the Thames with raw sewage after torrential rain. As the great sage of Manchester, James Royle, once put it: 'Immortality, my arse!'. The body is a mechanism that is wearing out. In the land beyond change there are changing rooms, where it's impossible to conceal your beer gut and those greying chest hairs. The deep intelligence within your body is telling you that perpetual youth is a chimera; if only you will listen to this inner self-knowledge your life will be transformed. The land where everyone is old lives permanently within you. To accept mortality is to feel the breath of the cosmos over your shoulder. And it's suffering from a bad case of halitosis.

In practice: Beyond your body
Let us try to remove the assumption that your body is not ageing just because various self-help gurus say that wrinkles have no place in a cosmos where we are constantly remaking ourselves according to a timeless paradigm. Do not get a life. Listen to your time-bound soul and get a death. The old git paradigm teaches us that existence is ever

changing and that at the end of it we die anyway. Habit is the enemy of ageing. To age properly we must accept new ways of thinking and believing and then embrace decrepitude and entropy.

The exercises I have devised here are designed to help you reinterpret your world view so that you can accept the inevitability of burgeoning nasal hair and out-of-control follicles rampaging within and on your ears. To have an old body you need to receive new experiences and absorb new perceptions. You must be fully aware of the inner level of decay within your ageing soul.

EXERCISE 1: Seeing through the reality of your timeless foot
Simply hold your foot out in front of you. That one with the sticking plaster on the big toe from where you dropped a kitchen knife into it while attempting to cut the bread. The sticking plaster has a small patch of dried blood on it and is fraying at the edges. Look at the lines and scuffed bits of scaly skin on your sole and examine them closely.

This foot appears to be made of flesh, muscle and bone. Bits of white flaky skin are falling off it. But let us imagine we are looking at your foot through a powerful microscope. Beyond the flesh there are cells joined together by bits of something or other, probably microscopic lumps of Blu Tack. These cells are comprised of atoms. While in turn, these sub-atomic particles are divided into electrons, protons and neutrons. Here, matter and energy collide and we are in quantum space. It is a world beyond space, time, Doctor Who, dimensions and sticking plaster.

Now let us take a return journey through all the infinitesimally small sub-divisions of matter back to the reality of a human foot. You are still knackered and your foot is still getting older. That sticking plaster is still there and still fraying and losing its stickability. Soon it will have fallen off and turn up on your bathroom floor. It is a cosmic metaphor for your life.

Reflect upon this exercise and consider its implications:

- Every solid particle of matter is composed of big bits of empty space. That's a lot of nothingness. Hell, even Scotland isn't that empty.

- If we penetrate deep enough into the heart of matter and energy we discover God; only to find that He doesn't take cold calls.

- The gap between two electrons is pretty damn big. Or pretty small. Depending on which way you look at it, really. Particularly for those of us who don't know what an electron is.

Take a look at your foot again. That foot is yours and at the quantum level it is pure creative potential. Only sadly, we do not live in the quantum world. Take a look at those crusty bits of the sole. You need to see a chiropodist. In the human dimension it is the foot of an old git.

EXERCISE 2: Mind the gap

Take a candle out in to your garden. Hold it up against a star in the night sky. You might like to play a Cat Stevens CD while doing this to help transcend the non-quantum universe. The candle and star might seem to be billions of miles apart, but everything at the quantum level is connected by photon torpedoes of light, waves of electromagnetic energy and, erm, lots of other stuff. Carefully wipe your glasses. Thanks to your myopia everything in the universe really does look rather similar.

Think about the lessons you have learned from this exercise:

- Every part of your body is part of the active quantum field. Each cell is comprised of information, energy and a few squiggly bits; we are the cells of the universe.

- Nothing is separate in the wholeness of the universe. Everything in the universe is part of the quantum field. At the end of the universe is a hedgerow.

- When dating new age types it is always best to play the quantum field.

- Maybe you should attend that check-up at the opticians.

EXERCISE 3: Heavy breathing

Sit in a comfortable chair and listen to your breath. It's sounding a bit asthmatic, isn't it? You are wheezy and you could do with some cough medicine. Close your eyes and try to get in touch with your quantum energy levels. Gently inhale and feel the air move through your lungs. Imagine that the air you are inhaling is from a star on the other side of the universe. It may help to recall images from Star Trek for this.

Feel the power of that air inside you as you inhale. It feels cosmic, doesn't it? Try chewing a Galaxy bar as a study aid, or if that fails a Mars bar. Feel the unity between humanity, God, the Universe and your back garden. But don't tread in next door's cat's poo while you are doing this and watch out for mosquitoes. This will help reconnect you with the quantum field and take you a breath closer to eternal old age.

EXERCISE 4: New words for old souls
Now you have absorbed the fact that your body is stuck in space and time, redefine yourself through saying these statements out aloud (although not on the bus or train in case you get funny looks from early-morning commuters).

Through my new awareness I can now accept and experience a body that is:

- Owing instead of growing

- Chewing instead of renewing

- Rigid instead of supple

- Fat instead of thin

- Well-oiled instead of fluid

- Drinking hot chocolate instead of making love

- Time-bound instead of timeless

- Buggered if it can haul itself to the gym anymore

- Losing all interest in personal grooming.

Further sets of defining aphorisms that you might like to repeat to yourself or bore your friends with include:

- I am the sum of my atoms and cells and they are past their cell-by-date

- I am my thoughts and I am losing my power of concentration

- I am my ego and it is becoming more difficult to control the older I get. I am becoming increasingly cantankerous

- I am beyond timelessness; my time-bound self is ageing and tired and in need of a good lie down.

Repeating these statements will provide your body with vital new assumptions about itself. The human body is little more than an answerphone full of messages that go on too long and which you've forgotten to rewind. Let us wipe that tape clean and start with a new outgoing message. Let the imprints of the past be gone. This new information flow will provide carpet slippers for the new old soul.

Urgent new biological information about how embarrassing it is when the hairs around your private parts start to turn grey will redefine your body's sense of self and help it travel beyond the old ageless paradigm. Your body's cells are now receiving new programming and all without having to ring up a hugely expensive computer helpline. Your software isn't up to sexual misadventures any more and your hard drive is corrupted. You are heading into the realm of the time-bound sage who acknowledges his own mortality. The gap is narrowing between your old self and your new self. Soon you will be the joyful host of an ageing body and confused mind.

CHAPTER 2
AWARENESS OF MORTALITY

Ageing depends on awareness. The human mind is a tremendously powerful vehicle; it is the juggernaut of cosmic consciousness. Thoughts are more powerful than boulders. What we believe conditions how our cells will react in the space/time field. If we believe that we are forever young we will be stuck in the hopeless cycle of visits to the gym, pursuing younger partners in the illusion that we are still fit, virile, desirable sexual beings and listening to hip-hop and dance trance throughout our lives. Only when we can lose the illusion of the inevitability of hair-colouring and face lifts and accept the gifts of ugliness can we truly understand our position in the unity that is the universe.

In the old paradigm we were responding to old preconceptions, to learned behaviour that dictated we were all young in our hearts. In the old belief system we grew up believing that youth was inevitable, that we could travel the world during our retirement and climb mountains in our 90s.

The unsustainable nature of perpetual youth

Once people had the innate sense to become old at 30. But today the illusion of youth has conquered every aspect of our awareness.

Consider the example of your dear old mum and dad. Do they still wear denim? Do they insist their grandchildren call them by their first names rather than Nan and Granpa? Are they listening to rock music and smoking marijuana? Have they recently gone topless on a Spanish beach or suggested a naturist holiday just to show how young and liberated they are? Do they have noisy and embarrassing sex while you are sleeping in the next room just to prove that old people still have active sex lives?

They live a youthful lifestyle because of societal expectations; yet all the time their souls are craving the release of grumpiness, deafness, dementia and slothful indifference. One of the great Indian sages once said: 'People stay young because they hear other old people listening to rock CDs. Yet inside their souls is the Zimmer frame of eternity.' Youth is an illusion, a chimera for our times.

William Shakespeare wrote that at the end of the seven ages of man we end up in 'second childishness and mere oblivion/Sans teeth, sans eyes, sans taste, sans everything.' And if anything the great Bard was being optimistic. Remember, he was writing in an age before old codgers tried to understand email and the Internet, clogging up chat rooms and never quite understanding how to perform a force quit or set their date and time preferences.

The new belief system must be based on the premise that we are trapped in a body that is doomed to age. Hair that is black will later be grey. To touch our true old selves we must rid our minds of false consciousness from the old paradigm and accept these statements:

- Oldness is inevitable. It happens. It's always happened. The dinosaurs survived for millions of years but eventually they got old and died. Neanderthal man had a life expectancy of about two years and then ended up in the belly of a sabre-toothed tiger. Neolithic man suffered terrible arthritis from carrying all those standing stones about and then trying to get them to stand up straight. The Roman Emperors got old and corrupt and the Empire crumbled. OK, today we live a bit longer, but at the end of the day we get old and die. Always have done, always will.

- Oldness is normal. Beneath every piece of cosmetic surgery lies cellulite, blubber, chicken necks and wizened hands. Inside every young person there is an old codger waiting to get out.

- Oldness is annoying. Work on your acceptance of this fact. Encourage an innate sense of irritation at getting old and decrepit. You end up preferring tea to sex. Arthritis hurts. That 25-year-old on the football pitch makes you look like a slowing idiot. No one fancies you anymore. You end up saying that you can't hear the words of any of this new-fangled music.

- Oldness is universal. The cosmos is one gigantic struggle between the forces of creation and destruction. And you have picked the losing ticket.

- Death is fatal. There's no one in history who has not died. Ever. Apart from maybe Jesus Christ, but even He gave up after an extra three days and took early retirement at the age of 33.

Human life spans appear to be increasing. But so-called longevity is merely the flowing of time which may go backwards, forwards or do a couple of somersaults and then stand still. If life is a river then you are still going to get washed out to sea. You live a bit longer but you still die.

As I tell the deluded middle-aged people who arrive at my surgery on their motorbikes and rollerblades, there is nothing inevitable about youth. You do not have to wear knee pads into middle-age.

It is always necessary to investigate the lifestyle of someone who feels they are perpetually young. When people come to see me at my holistic ageing practice with what they believe to be signs of terminal youthfulness, it is striking how often they are confusing the symptoms of youthfulness with those of physical fitness. I am not seeing young people at all. I am seeing fit people.

An apparently simple action such as going to the gym can mimic all the symptoms of youthfulness. Watching MTV on that infernal set that's always on, drinking copious amounts of bottled mineral water or isotonic fluids, admiring that person in the tight Lycra doing the leg presses, inviting strangers to feel your pecs, the lowering of blood pressure, pounding on treadmills on that perpetual marathon to nowhere, offering to join in a game of five-a-side football when they put out a request for an extra player on the PA, relishing the sweat oozing from your saturated running top – these are all symptoms that are commonly associated with the cult of youth. Yet exactly the same symptoms describe a person who is fit.

Western doctors have long been ascribing these symptoms, such as sound blood pressure and pulse rates, solid muscle posture, lack of fatty tissue, healthy heart rates and the like, as mere signs of youthfulness. It is only when we take a holistic approach to the patient that we realise that he or she is not young but merely fit. Most of our body is water; at the quantum level it contains vast areas of nothingness. Cells die, they renew themselves, they try to do sit-ups but can't be bothered, eat too many crisps and they get old. With some careful tweaking of a subject's lifestyle we can release the ageing body trapped inside the prison of a svelte athlete.

Negating youthfulness through sloth

Lack of exercise can reverse nearly all of the negative effects of youthfulness. With a programme of applied slothfulness, your life expectancy can drop by at least 20 years. Physical inactivity can accentuate the inner pensioner in all of us. When an attitude of positive enlightenment towards ageing is adopted and physical inactivity is embraced, then the human body can actively deteriorate as we use it. The following factors can all help advance a previously fit person towards a blissful state of oldness, where he or she is absolutely content with senility and feebleness:

• Eating nothing but pea soup

• Never opening a bottle of whisky unless you intend to finish it

• Sitting around watching videos all day or better still watching daytime television

- Driving to the bus stop

- Eating peanut butter on toast for breakfast, minus the toast

- Smoking 50 fags a day

- Replacing your water intake with caffeine

- Listening to CDs by recommended old-age holistic artists such as Leonard Cohen, Morrissey and Bob Dylan. These will encourage a sense of misery and enable you to find and then balance your inner curmudgeon.

Let me put this another way. In the old paradigm, the hypothetical subject A might have a biological age of 50 but act like B who has a biological age of 30, who in turn behaves like C, who has a biological age of 20. But once we acknowledge that linear time is running out and accept the inevitability of oldly going on a one-way journey to the grave with our loved ones haggling over who pays the funeral bills, then the respective hypothetical subjects take the chronological order of ABC, easy as 123.

The habits and programming of youth culture must be changed for the new paradigm. Some of the worst symptoms displayed by those who refuse to acknowledge their biological age are a sense of contentment with their work, sex and social lives. These people tend to take pleasure in their daily routines. The only way we can overcome this powerful societal programming is to cultivate a more positive philosophy of resentment. Below is a list of some useful pointers towards successful ageing.

Positive factors that retard youthfulness

- Extreme dissatisfaction with your employment, dislike of the working hours, the office culture, the pot plants, the team building exercises, the coffee machine, the late payment of your salary and in particular the knowledge that your boss, who is half your age, is an overpromoted nonentity with all the personality of an automated switchboard.

- Preferring golf to sex

- Drinking as much as you can because you're a long time dead

- Never taking a lunch break because the others will think you are slacking

- Never taking a holiday, because the others will think you can't keep up

- Hollering at the kids/cats/dogs when you are late for work and can't find your diary and where are your sodding shoes and how did they get under the sofa?

- Blaming your spouse for any object in the house that is lost

- Building up £90,000 of debts on 16 credit cards, which your partner has no idea exist

- Complete failure to understand modern music

- A sense of impotent rage whenever you see your sports team in action and an annoying habit of turning to the young person next to you and complaining that the players of 30 years ago were nothing like these overpaid wingeing prima donnas

- Playing bingo

- Buying net curtains instead of blinds

- Living in Morecambe

- Trying to book a ticket for the cinema on an automated ticket telephone line

- Going on coach tours to popular holiday destinations where your itinerary is strictly controlled and every meal planned in advance, so that you don't receive anything too challenging or foreign. It is very important for the successful old codger to eschew all forms of independent travel

- Looking endlessly at maps and going over and over projected routes

Negative factors that encourage youthfulness

- Gymnasiums

- MTV

- Viagra

- Hair dye

- Cosmetic surgery

- Cliff Richard

- Sex

- Enjoyment of occupation

- Writing books or composing operas after retirement age

- Pop festivals

- Denim

- Cycling

- Music magazines marketed at the over-40s

- Mini-breaks on low-budget airlines

- Speed dating for divorcees

- Daytime TV agony aunts

- Hair transplants/extensions

- All forms of born again religious fervour and associated incessant smiling

- Self-help books

- Travel magazines

- Leather jackets

- Lycra

- Evening classes

- Radio 2

- Designer sunglasses

- Agony aunts on daytime TV

- The Rolling Stones

Adapt and decline

Another major factor in finding a practical alternative to staying young is a lack of adaptability. It can be very distressing to watch a young person refuse to give up on life. Old people have no problem in doing this. The terminally young at heart believe that if they keep themselves centred, balance the yin and yang in their lives, juggle balls during moments of stress (while irritating all around them because grown adults just shouldn't do juggling, that's the job of medieval court jesters) and always maintain a delicate balance between creative and destructive, positive and negative forces, the energy of their life force will be maintained.

Youth is in the mind. In 2004 Dr Fred Smeggins and his team at Harvard took a control group of thirty 60-year-olds on a weekend trip to a seaside resort. The pensioners all regarded themselves as 'grey panthers', travelling all over the world and leading active and often downright perverted sex lives. Yet for that weekend Dr Smeggins insisted that the subjects must act as if it was 1969. The only subjects that could be discussed were those in the papers of that year, and the only music played was by the likes of Bob Dylan, Joan Baez and Jimi Hendrix.

Within hours the control group had started to display a range of psychological responses that suggested they were no longer comfortable with their youthful attitudes. They had started to remember just how difficult it was to score acid at Woodstock, how horrible the veggie burgers tasted, and how bad the festival loos and the sound quality on transistor radios was back then. Some began to hyperventilate as repressed memories of adolescent heavy petting re-emerged. In the months after the experiment the subjects began to actively think of themselves as old. They allowed the grey in their hair to flourish and many men eschewed pony-tails in favour of short back and sides haircuts. Some even began to wear patterned jumpers, golf shoes and shapeless blue raincoats.

We have to believe in old age to positively acknowledge it. A famous study by Professor Bert Postlethwaite of Neasden University revealed that those senior citizens who have found true irascibility tend to be those who are least adaptable to change. Changes is a record by David Bowie. You do not want changes in your life. If there must by any change, then adapt to it sullenly and with much grouching. The master of decrepitude must work at maintaining a rigid posture in this world of glad-to-be-grey pensioners. You can test your rigidity rating by completing the simple questionnaire opposite, awarding yourself a point for every one of these statements you agree with.

INADAPTABILITY QUESTIONNAIRE

1. If your computer experiences software glitches do you bang the mouse until it breaks?
2. Does the fact that the computer helpline costs 50 pence a minute make you break out in heavy sweating every time you phone those overpaid student geeks stealing your hard-earned money?
3. Do you feel that there's nothing wrong in your life that being 30 couldn't put right?
4. You never vote because it only encourages them.
5. You kick any person in a luminous jacket that approaches you on a street corner asking you to spare just five minutes to take out a standing order for a deserving charity.
6. Children annoy the hell out of you.
7. You are always right.
8. Getting old entails a long period of sitting around waiting to die.
9. You never recovered from the death of your pet hamster when you were five.
10. Everyone in business is always trying to screw you over.
11. If asked to do something for nothing your first question is always 'What's in it for me?'
12. God is dead.

If you scored:

9–12 points: Excellent. You are completely rigid in your thinking and can therefore grow old in abject misery while really annoying young people.

4–8 points: You still have some work to do on your rigidity awareness. You spend too much time empathizing with other people and attempting to understand their point of view. Remember, they are not to be trusted and everyone else is out to get you.

0–3 points: You write self-help books on alternatives to growing old.

A huge number of the symptoms of youthfulness can be traced to the modern fads of fitness training, alcohol awareness and emotional intelligence. It is only through enhanced awareness that we can experience the reversal of youth. Energy and information must be re-ordered and the destructive habits of youth eradicated. True liberation of the mind, soul and body can only be found in the freedom to dribble down your shirt at meal times and shout at kids playing ball games in the street.

Yet youthfulness is like an addiction. The longer the years of programming, the more difficult it is for the individual to rid themselves of self-destructive youthful attitudes. To overcome youth we must concentrate our attention on the field of awareness.

Personal change can breach the tyranny of youth. We can change everything within us. We can even change our underpants. White

Y-fronts, seldom if ever changed, are much better than boxer shorts for the old man. Let us look at some ways of using our intention to alter the old ways of conditioning.

In practice: Utilizing the power of oldness

Our bodies are governed by intention. All space-time events in the quantum field are manifestations of the energy and information that we allow to flow through our bodies. If we allow elderly energy to flow through our bodies at the cellular level, then we can overcome youthful vitality and restore the rightful balance to our bodies. Let us try to find the new pathway towards decrepitude, deafness and slip-on shoes.

EXERCISE 1: Paying attention to your buttocks

Find a quiet place away from the sound of police sirens and drug raids. Lock the kids in their bedrooms. Now close your eyes and sit in your most comfortable armchair. Holding the TV remote might help relax those who are still struggling to match their awareness to the field. Now clench your buttocks and imagine you are doing a series of 100 sit-ups with a personal fitness trainer bawling in your ear. Then let the buttocks relax and imagine that you are watching your favourite soap opera on TV or your favourite episode of first generation Star Trek, that really good one where Spock has a beard in a parallel universe. You are now free of distortions in the field. Feel the energy transform your buttock muscles from taut and firm to flabby and ageing. Your body will immediately feel a sensation of comfort as it relaxes into the cushions. Now order a take-away pizza. You are starting to experience the field; you are on the pathway to the land where everyone is old and no one gives a sod about it.

EXERCISE 2: Transcending youthfulness

Lie down with your eyes closed and imagine the scene of great joy when it first occured to you that you were getting old. It might be the moment you realized that fashion didn't affect you any more or the time you realized that it was OK to stop buying music papers. Or the occasion where you discovered your preference for staying in and drinking a can of beer in front of the telly because bars are full of noisy people and passive smoking and you couldn't be bothered with the crush on the train home. Or the time you bought a home brew kit because you could brew beer for three pence a pint at home and that way you could be as anti-social as you wanted and you wouldn't have to talk to anyone in a pub. Focus on that moment and your biorhythms will remember it too. They will start to feel the onrush of oldness and a time when to be feeble is to be empowered because pumping weights at 55 is just plain ridiculous.

Everything is in the continuity of the field. If you focus intention and awareness you can train your cells to grow old. If you listen to your inner intelligence then the outcome of ageing can be achieved simply through intention. Your body will listen to your intentions; in the old paradigm, you were ignoring your body's plea for peace and a non-existent sex life. But now your biorhythms are responding, you can reach the place where the inner old git may flourish. Say to yourself that you intend to be:

• Older and grumpier

• Inarticulate and bumbling

- The sort of person who can never find their glasses case

- Rude and irascible

- As unfit as possible

- A silly old bugger who irritates the neighbours and argues about fence boundaries.

The reality underlying every aspect of our existence is decay. Today only a very few people have managed to roll back the cycle of destructive youth, but for those who have in every case the process has certain common qualities:

1. What we, in the scientific profession, refer to as 'a right result' was sought.

2. As the five sages known as the Spice Girls once pleaded – showing a profound awareness of the transience of modern youthful civilisation disguised in the trappings of a mere pop lyric – 'tell me what you want, what you really really want.' In every case that I have studied where individuals moved towards successful oldness, the intention was precise and the person was sure about exactly what they wanted.

3. The people involved were not concerned about the physical processes involved in regaining their sense of advanced age, they 'just wanted to bloody well do it'.

4. There was no doubt in the souls of those who changed themselves. Doubt is a self-fulfilling prophecy of failure and condemns the doubter to a life spent drinking mineral water while pacing treadmills to nowhere in the MTV-sound tracked, aerobic-obsessed prison of the soul known as the gymnasium.

5. Once we fulfil one intention successfully then we are much better equipped to fulfil our future intentions. Old thoughts breed old actions.

6. What happened felt as natural as taking out a Thermos flask of insipid brown tea on a day trip to the beach. It was an extension of the subject's inner intelligence focused on becoming an aged, blithering old fool.

7. When the outcome of acceptable oldness was achieved, there was no doubt that it had been achieved through a conscious force that embodies a larger unifying reality. Some call this force God, fate, self, bad luck, the quantum field, Buddha, Jesus, Lord or just Brian. All these names are acceptable for our purpose. There is one huge all-encompassing intelligence that is willing us all on, uniting with us to fulfil our desire and intentions to be old.

We can all intend to improve our ageing processes. In terms of our physical and mental senses, some deterioration can be achieved every day. Note anything that impairs your youthfulness and act upon it the next day. Maybe one day you will leave a ring on the hob on, or forget that your washing has been festering in the washing machine for the past three days. Every channel towards dodderiness should be explored. Tell yourself that today I intend to be:

- More lethargic

- Less creative

- Less alert

- More mendacious

- More likely to dribble my food

- Seeking continual physical and mental deterioration.

Listen to the internal signals from every atom, every cell, every pore of your body. What you wish for can be achieved. Your creative intelligence has the answer. Forgetfulness and misanthropy lie within your own mind and body. Intention, awareness and intelligence can combine to at last allow us the right to be old.

Chapter 3
Encouraging Entropy

All life forces in our universe are subject to entropy. Everything falls apart, including you. Entropy is really just a fancy way of saying that everything in the universe is prone to degeneration, decay, destruction, dissolution and lots of other words beginning with 'd'.

The human body is subjected to the same forces as every other space/time event in the quantum field. I am writing these words while contemplating my compost bin, which doesn't half give off a nasty whiff. Ancient potatoes sprout tentacles before slowly turning to mush; onions go green and squelchy; carrots grow white mould; coffee grinds merge with egg shells; blackening banana skins fuse with bits of orange peel and festering spinach; beans become semi-liquid; cabbages go all yellow and gooey.

Yet from all this decay springs the creative force of life. You should see the fruit flies that swarm out of the thing every time the lid is lifted. Those worms are big and juicy and wriggly. Even the odd snail thrives down there. Open up the hatch at the bottom of the composter and there is lovely black organic fertilizer, ready to bring life to the roses in my garden. Destruction and creation are all part of the same unity. It's just that in the ageing human body you're at the top of the compost bin rather than the bottom.

The Universe is really just one gigantic compost bin. It started off as primeval soup and one day we will all be in the quantum soup kitchen again. The Earth will become galactic mulch. Even planets, stars and galaxies are doomed to ultimate destruction. Stars think they're pretty clever, but they get swallowed up by black holes and zapped into anti-matter universes where all they ever get is the odd visit from Captain Kirk.

There's nothing we can do about entropy and our coming destruction. So let's hasten it on a bit and enjoy our ultimate decay. Our kids can do all that creative stuff. But us old 'uns are knackered. One day we will be providing fertilizer for trees. What's the point in prolonging your life when all those organic molecules in the soil need a good feed? Human ashes scattered over the land provide valuable nutrients for the ever-abundant circle of life. Let us encourage death and decay and our remorseless march towards a semi-vegetative state. Entropy is to embraced in the new paradigm.

The power of decrepitude

I shall refer to the mysterious dark force pulsing through our veins as decrepitude. All things are heading towards chaos. Yet within the wonderful mechanism that is our body there is an inner intelligence, a creative power that realises the value of decrepitude at work. The body knows that when it reaches a certain age it is only dignified to develop wrinkles and crow's feet, varicose veins and ingrowing toenails. DNA registers that it has been passed on to the next generation and the only sensible thing for the ageing human to do now is get old, get drunk and then die.

Energy can never be destroyed, it can only change form. With a bit of luck, one day your atoms might form a piece of lichen in the Lake District. Life must flow towards death. At a cellular level it is time to dissolve yourself, to scatter the corporeal form on the winds of the quantum field and feel the breath of eternal ageing within your being.

So much depends on finding the right balance in our lives. We are tightrope walkers between forces of youth and ageing, suspended above the cosmic abyss. People start to suffer from prolonged youthfulness when the innate balance within the body is askew.

Your entire body is full of awareness. Your cells are influenced by every thought, even that one you just had about shall I close this book or not. And when we ignore our awareness, even when it is saying that no grown human of 45 years of age should be listening to Eminem and claiming to enjoy it because really it's the same attitude as punk, our bodies go into a potentially fatal state of imbalance.

An out-of-balance body may never show the proper signs of ageing. This may result in numerous symptoms such as low blood pressure, happy family life, contented employment, enhanced motor functions and low alcohol consumption without the victim of youth ever realizing that something is wrong. We are sleepwalking towards the perpetual unhappiness of permanent youth.

The truly balanced person will realise that there are several irreversible markers of old age:

- Your muscles and dangly bits sag horribly

- You and your partners have separate library books on your separate bedside tables

- You wear pyjamas in bed and when you get up at night you put fluffy slippers on your feet

- Proximity to the loo during the night becomes more important than who is in your bed

- You get lard-arsed

- You love watching property, cookery, gardening and make-over programmes on TV

- You perceive yourself to be past caring, unattractive, boring and staid

- You start telling kids that in your day you could leave your door open and no one ever burgled you and if anyone misbehaved he just got a clip round the ear from the friendly bobby on the beat and you should know because you are a boring old bastard.

Strength in sitting

Idleness can be very helpful in restoring balance to the body and encouraging the state of entropy. Old people do not do; the sage old person simply sits and complains. Idleness and sloth can help restore order to a body that is suffering the chronic imbalances created by health food shops, muesli, tofu and general physical fitness.

Holistically we can define the creation of ordered linear time from youthful delusions of timelessness in this simple equation:

excess + insomnia + obsessiveness + inactivity = BALANCE

A number of simple lifestyle changes can enable an individual to lead a balanced life, where he or she is hastening on towards entropy without the illusion of youth. Following these habits can diminish your lifespan by as much as 20 years. These include:

- Drinking espresso coffee followed by a cigarette and nothing else for breakfast

- Staying up all night watching Canadian tree-felling competitions on cable TV

- Snacking whenever you can

- Getting bladdered, ratted, sloshed, pissed, inebriated or in a generally crapulous state every weekend

- Eating as much red meat, eggs, cheese and milk as you can find

- Practising the art of physical inactivity in a place where you can safely channel hop.

Your body's inner intelligence responds to the messages you send it. Hearing someone say 'Come at me tiger, take me now big boy!' can induce all kinds of changes at the molecular level in many males. Cells enlarge, engorge and show evidence of electrical charges boosting levels of alertness and increased capacity to espouse feminist ideals and leave the loo seat down, all guided by the supreme intelligence vested within our veins. A man's cells have been proved to respond to such stimuli even when the person saying these words is on the other end of an Internet connection.

Such words act as the programming for our bodies and affect our field of awareness. This is why we must be very careful how we use the words young and old. When we say the words 'You're as young as the woman/man you feel' or phrases like 'Youth is an attitude not an age', we are sending messages to our body at the cellular level saying that youth is attainable even when you are at an age when you should be trimming the hedge and drinking cocoa before an early bedtime.

This is why in the new paradigm we must learn to communicate with our inner intelligence through awareness enforced by positive messages. If asked to try rock climbing in middle age just reply 'Why, I'm far too old to do that, how about a game of darts instead?'. Try waking up each morning and saying 'I will never enjoy myself again!' and you will find it strangely empowering.

Remember that youth and age are opposites:

- Clarity is bad, senility is oh, I forget now

- The young live for the moment, we live in the past

- Youth is full of temporary excitement, old age is characterized by an enlightened sense of permanent boredom

- The young possess beauty, we oldsters possess love handles

- Young people believe in tomorrow, old people believe in yesterday.

The perfect cycle of oldness

Some individuals have composed symphonies or produced great works of art in their 90s. Others have run marathons and climbed tower blocks on rope harnesses. But do you really want to be working into your dotage? The message your body is transmitting to your mind is that every cell in your body is moving towards entropy. Listen to your body's inner cycle. Its cycle should be naturally balanced, with its metaphorical tyres pumped up and a luminous green sash and helmet waiting in the hallway, encouraging you to move inexorably towards old age.

Nature has the natural cycles of the seasons, lunar cycles affect the tides on Earth and bicycles are essential for old ladies going to church. Menstrual cycles affect women's hormone production and allow them to be irritable towards their partners when they forgot to buy the tea bags or put the recycling out; at an intuitive level the body's hormones are directing women towards irritability as the precursor of the blissful grumpiness of old age.

Intelligence flows through everything we do. Our biorhythms are the chiming of the body's internal symphony. They tell us the correct balance for ageing disgracefully. For maximum efficiency we must follow the body's biorhythms as they pulse through our lives urging us onwards towards the true knowledge of feebleness and forgetfulness.

Consider carefully the biorhythms of your body and the messages they are sending to your brain. Compile a timetable for your day and try to adhere to it. Morning is best for reading the paper; midday is the optimum time for armchair sitting and then topping up on salt levels by buying crisps at the corner shop; afternoon sees a peak period for the gentle watching of daytime TV quiz shows with attractive women offering up vowel letters; early evening sees the body at its most receptive for a heavy weight-inducing meal and for easy repetitive tasks such as drinking several beers in succession; midnight to daylight sees an increasing alertness in the older body and is the ideal time for making phone calls complaining about neighbours' noisy parties.

The essence of the body's balanced biorhythms can be expressed in the following equation:

Morning   = breakfast TV
Noon   = lunch
Afternoon = snooze and daytime TV
Evening = repeats of the Antiques Roadshow
Night   = warm malted drink followed by an early bedtime

It is very important that we do not forget about stress but try to carry with us the memory of stress. If you are an ambulance driver try to remember every wounded body you have ever seen and carry that with you when you finish your shift. Aim at increased blood pressure and heart palpitations, so that the recollection of stress is more stressful than the original event.

Because the body naturally tries not to remember stress, its balance can easily be thrown. Clearly there is something wrong at a fundamental level in the human body when it cannot respond sufficiently to stress. We should be receiving stress with joy; it is the ultimate liberator of the old soul. Stress should be like petrol entering the internal combustion engine of your very being. The young person who is free of stress can experience a number of maladies, including dynamism, optimism, desires to change the world, enter politics or start up a dot.com company.

When we are young, stress occurs, but the body rapidly returns to a stress-free position. This can be expressed with a simple diagram (see opposite). Each dot signifies one of the vital balancing indicators of the body. When we are young they start in a level state, are briefly disrupted by stress, but all shift back to the same position after stress is encountered (fig. 1). It is when the middle-aged person's vital bodily indicators still return to their starting position that we find all the problems that result in a tragic refusal to age (fig. 2). It is only when these indicators refuse to return to their original position and start to move around all over the place that we have attained true balance for the body (fig. 3).

FIGURE 1

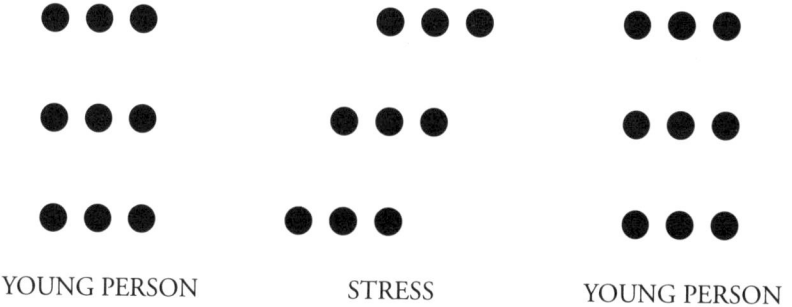

YOUNG PERSON   STRESS   YOUNG PERSON

FIGURE 2

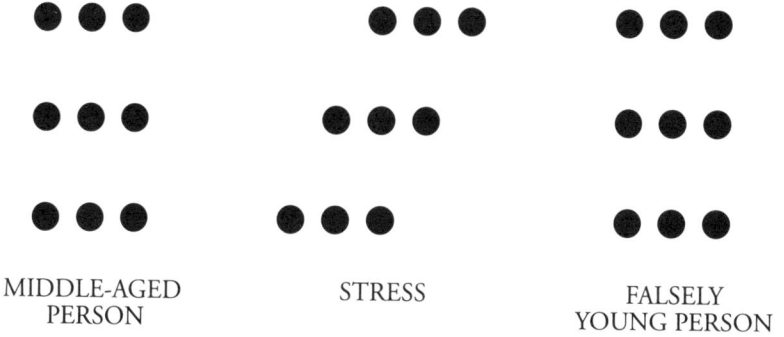

MIDDLE-AGED   STRESS   FALSELY
PERSON   YOUNG PERSON

FIGURE 3

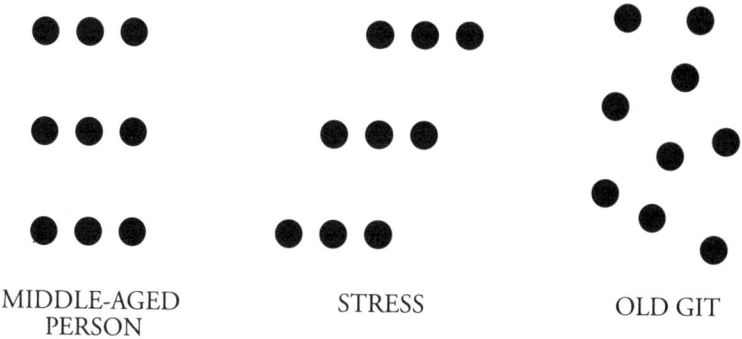

MIDDLE-AGED   STRESS   OLD GIT
PERSON

The body's essential need for stress

The biggest hindrance to successful ageing is a lack of stress in your life. George Orwell once wrote that by the time a man is 50 he has the face he deserves. We should not want some fresh-faced characterless visage when we have reached a half century of fulfillment on the journey towards silver oblivion. The passing of time is in its own way the beautiful music of the cosmos. Wrinkles are to be celebrated. Grey jowls, bags under the eyes, liver spots, blotches, skin problems, urticaria, halitosis, hearing aids: all are signs of the successful individual who is not afraid to listen to their internal biorhythms and embrace ageing.

It must be remembered that it is not just experiencing stress that is important but our response to stress that matters so much. Hopefully an experience of stress will bring forth memories of other stresses, the body will go in to its fight or flight response, and lots of stress hormones will be released, speeding the body on towards visible signs of ageing.

Work longer hours, downsize more of your staff, live off caffeine, spit at charity collectors, be horrible to your partners and then dump them for no reason: all these attitudes will help attain the lived-in face of the successful person who is old before their time.

Stress is the stepping stone towards sublime ageing. The more stress you can experience the more your body will be guided by its natural biorhythms towards eternal ageing. A truly stressed individual can look at least 20 years older than their biological age and glide towards true cantankerousness. We can only be our true old selves in the realm beyond youthful delusion.

Simple ways of generating stress

Moving to the city can be an excellent generator of stress. You might consider London, New York, Tokyo, Beijing, Baghdad, Chernobyl or anywhere in the third world with an unstable economy and government. Try to pick a city with the worst air quality readings and most noise pollution. Live on a main road if possible or better still near an airport. If you have children, take up a demanding job where the employers hate anyone who has kids and demand that you work excessive hours with impossible deadlines.

Remember though that in cities people in orange robes will sometimes accost you on the street and try to entice you in to meditation sessions, perhaps with the offer of free food. Beware the cult of calm. Calm is the illusion which feeds the mirage of perpetual youth. Meditation is to be avoided as it has been proved to lower stress levels. If you do find yourself trapped in a meditation session adopt a holistic approach to the problem, listen to your inner voice and think to yourself: 'This is not pure awareness at all, it's actually pretty bloody boring sitting here listening to my breath and trying to shut out the police sirens outside. I think I'll go down the pub instead.'

The great benefit of urban life is that in cities people shout at other road users while sitting in traffic jams, they sound their horns at anyone who happens to stall their engine, they feel like punching out traffic wardens, resent the invasion of their body space on underground trains, take a continual buffeting from huge backpacks belonging to people on their gap year and spend hours trying to hail cabs home in the rain after midnight. All this can have an extremely beneficial effect on your body's natural balance, releasing valuable stress hormones and countering the body's previous tendency towards enthusiastic youthfulness.

The positive energy of anger
When experiencing stress it is important to try to trigger memories of past stresses. These memories can help us age internally.

• If a traffic warden is giving you a ticket after your parking meter ran out a mere 30 seconds ago, try to remember all the other wardens who have ever given you parking tickets and recall your feelings of rage and utter impotence and how that appeal was a waste of time as they doubled the fine anyway.

• Never leave sufficient time to drive or take the train to a really important football match. Leave at the last possible moment ensuring that you miss the kick off, can't buy a programme and have to run the last half an hour to the stadium. Try to support a team that is useless so that your side will be at least two goals down when you do finally sit down.

• When travelling on a train pick the most crowded compartment and never rush for a seat. Stand up for as long as possible and try to position yourself near a rough sleeper who smells of stale urine and super strength lager.

- Try to place yourself in situations that are out of your control; confront crazy people who are wildly unpredictable and make sure you have no idea of their likely responses; ensure the only channel for your increasing frustration is excess eating and alcohol consumption.

Be aware of the sweat beneath your armpits, the reddening of your cheeks, the rapidity of your heartbeat and the throbbing between your temples as you slowly attune yourself to the inner intelligence that works within us all at the quantum level as we move towards the reality where everyone is old.

Ultimately we must link soul, mind and body on the path to entropy and fulfillment. The human body is like an old car that has a very poor carbon emission record and is about to fail its MOT again. Rust is all around you and soon you will be found in a field with grass growing through your bodywork. Remember, there are five essential assertions that youth cannot touch:

1. I am body. My body is pure, unalterable and sublime in its eternal knackeredness.

2. Everything is as it is meant to be. Our bodies are programmed to deteriorate at the cellulite level.

3. Certainty holds no fear for me. We get old, we die. So what? It's better than eternal life in the Bible Belt or Essex suburbs.

4. Life is a cosmic ceilidh dance. We have a few drinks, we take to the floor, we stand on someone's toes, we mess up the bit where we have to swing our partner to the left and go through the arch. Life flows, change meets non-change, we spend too much of our life in changing rooms.

5. Ageing is not a threat to me. It is my friend because it is under the control of an infinite creative power that knows that American dental work, as seen on TV shows where everyone is under 35, is mere self-delusion. Cosmetic surgery makes people look like mannequins. Bad teeth are infused with the breath of universal ageing. My life is moving towards awareness. We are all on the path to fulfillment through the acceptance that God plays dice, life is a game of random chance and at the end of it all we snuff it. We die decrepit, old and ugly.

In practice: Certainty is wisdom

The only certainty in life is death. Yet paradoxically life also appears to be full of uncertainty. Computers have system errors, employers make you redundant, US presidents nearly die in freak accidents swallowing pretzels, you can open a packet of crisps only to find the contents inside are soggy.

It is very important that we become angry about uncertainty. We must then respond to uncertainty with the familiar and reliable responses of rage, hurt and betrayal, emotions which all help release those valuable stress hormones. Only through anger can we open our awareness to the certainty of ageing.

Living in the past will help prevent the body falling into a falsely induced state of cellular rejuvenation. We must nurture a sense of sorrow and encourage the belief that things were always better in the past. Encourage the pessimism of the old soul who has seen too much and trusts no one. Never enjoy a ride at the funfair; instead focus on the poor safety records of certain fairground operatives and imagine your bloody headless body mangled beneath the big dipper.

Change is everywhere, loss is everywhere and it's extremely annoying to an old curmudgeon like you. Losing control whenever minor things irritate you is an important step in guiding your body towards the awareness of ageing. Feel threatened by everything. Get stressed. Look out all your old records by the Sex Pistols, The Clash, Stranglers, Stiff Little Fingers, Elvis Costello and the Dead Kennedys. Play them and start to feel really irate about everything. Turn the volume up full. Imagine you are Johnny Rotten meeting the Queen in 1977. Bang your head against the wall to records by Iron Maiden. Imagine you are a millionaire US white rap star from trailer trash stock who still has really serious issues with his mother. Take out videos of James Dean in *Rebel Without a Cause* or read *Look Back in Anger* by John Osborne. Nurture, hatred and bile. Behave like Jack Nicholson in *The Shining*. Let anger flow organically from every cell.

OUT-OF-CONTROL QUESTIONNAIRE

The person who is in control of their life will never age satisfactorily. Impotence is the initiator of wrinkles. To gauge just how out-of-control your life is answer the following questions. Award yourself one point for every statement you agree with:

1. I have never recovered from the traumas of my childhood. They screwed me up my mum and dad, and no amount of therapy will ever change that.
2. I sent ten bags of manure to my former spouse and his/her new partner.
3. I feel uncomfortable reading self-help books and dealing with holistic remedies.
4. I feel uncontrollable sexual urges towards my intern.
5. I believe that it is never too late to try magic mushrooms.
6. Dressing up in rubber and being dominated in a dungeon can really be quite good fun.
7. I quiz my grandchildren about their sex lives. Incessantly.
8. I no longer clean up my pet dog's poo with a pooper scooper. If someone is stupid enough to step in a dog turd it just makes my day.
9. The piano has been drinking, not me.
10. I agree with Quentin Crisp; the dust really doesn't get any thicker after seven years.

11. What is the point of walking? What is the point of reflection? Walking is a waste of time for people who don't have enough work to do.

12. The more money I spend on my grandchildren/children, the more I despise them.

13. I hate listening to other people droning on and on about their problems and wanting me to empathise with them.

14. It's really great to phone up the police and get someone nicked for a trivial offence. Especially if they are young.

15. There's a real thrill to be found in opening someone else's post.

16. When you're old it's really great as you can blame the fact you never clean the loo on your fading eyesight.

17. I'm very proud when people call me cynical.

18. I am irritable all the time. When I am in a pressurized situation I tend to lash out at people with my stick.

19. When I get involved in a row with my partner it's always really satisfying to bring up old arguments and everything that annoys me about them, particularly the way they always use their finger to open envelopes instead of the letter-opener.

20. I never use smokeless fuel in my fireplace even if I do live in a smoke-free zone. I burn wood, coal, toxin-laden plastic and self-help books instead.

If you scored:

19–20 points: Excellent. You are way out of control, uncomfortable with your inner feelings and intolerant of all around you. You will make an excellent old man/woman.

10–18 points: You are heading towards being out of control but still need to deal with repressed desires to be organised, efficient and on time.

0–9 points: You are concealing the hurt of leading a controlled, productive, emotionally aware life. The only emotion you can easily show is calm and serenity, yet this does not achieve what you really desire, which is to be a grumpy old sod, hated and loathed by everyone.

EXERCISE 1: Freeing your anger

All contrasting viewpoints should be interpreted as threats. Your body will then react with the 'fight or flight' stress response. If the person threatening you is smaller and weaker than yourself then fight the little twerp. Successful aggression in this situation will depend on your heightened sense of perception. These steps may prove useful:

1. I am right and the other person is an idiot. Always repeat these words to yourself in any conflict scenario.

2. My interpretation of events is absolutely correct.

3. This argument has to produce the outcome I want. There can be no room for compromise.

4. I am the victim! Get that? I am the victim here!

5. What is the other person involved in this argument feeling? I just don't care. All I want them to feel is pain.

6. There is no way this incident will ever help me. All my life I've been having raging arguments with people who have bumped into me in the supermarket aisle and it just proves what a horribly pointless thing life is.

Following the above steps creates space for spontaneous expressions of rage. While writing this book I missed the sleeper train to Scotland by 30 seconds thanks to a myopic and retarded cab driver and the most convoluted set of roadworks in the western world.

While experiencing a sense of lividness and impotent frustration, I said to myself 'Will this moment matter in a week's time?'. Inside me my awareness answered back 'Of course it will, you will still be as annoyed then as you are now'. Immediately stress signals surged through my body as I thought of the many other times I have missed flights and trains through my own tardiness and the sheer inefficiency of others. The old negative responses of stoicism had disappeared and my body was now showing the correct response of seeking solace through the over-consumption of alcohol until the morning train.

Accentuating old prejudices and denying access to new interpretations will hasten the transition to rigid-thinking irascible oldness. You will experience moments of stunning insight; you will realize 'I am old and I am a misanthropist. What do you intend to do about that, sonny?'.

EXERCISE 2: Peeling back the layers of youthfulness
There are many layers of youthfulness within your consciousness. We must peel these layers until we find the place deep within where everything hurts and the true awareness of our oldness lies. There is stillness inside yourself where everything is old. Write down these words:

I am perfect even when wearing bi-focal glasses. Everything in life is flowing towards the direction of a free bus pass. I am old.

Invariably people write this down and respond with inner thoughts of 'Nonsense, I've just bought a hip-hop CD!' or 'No! I've just copped off with someone who's 20 years younger than me!'. Some people might even jog around the block in sadly inappropriate young person's trainers while they are thinking this. Repeat this exercise ten times. The more you affirm this simple statement the more you will be guided towards an inner truth. The words 'I am old' may cause initial denial in you. But beyond even the most rigid conditioning there is a fundamental awareness that is screaming out to you 'I am old and I am starting to dribble! There are hairs growing out of my nose too!'. Being old is part of the essence of life. The statement 'I am old' is no longer buried in your subconscious; it is out there on the surface of your being demanding dentures and the right to misplace your boarding pass just before boarding a flight.

EXERCISE 3: Living in the past

The echoes from the past call us towards the land where everyone is old. Let the hurt of the past wash over the present and envelop you in the pleasing warmth of rigid thought. Never move on. Reconcile yourself with the joy of living with an acid heart. Psychiatrist Hugh Jarce broke down pain into separate categories:

- Pain in the past is painful

- The perception of pain in the future leads to perfect grumpiness

- Present pain leads to hurt

- The pain in Spain stays mainly on the plane.

To successfully experience oldness we must hold on to the hurt of the past and make sure that the young people of today suffer for it. Guilt, anger and depression must be allowed to flow through your being. Buy a walking stick even if you don't need it. Be bitter and tell long boring stories to your children about how there is no market in the world that can't go down as well as up and that the youth of today live in luxury compared to when you were young and no child ever had a television in their house let alone their room and what's wrong with walking to school and what are these Gameboy things they play with anyway? To inhabit the past is to inhabit a land where everything was always better. Living in the past can open the doors towards the permanent experience of the ageing body and the reality of the confused mind, which is always with you from now until senility.

CHAPTER 4
THE SCIENCE OF DECREPITUDE

Age is not simply a matter of longevity. To live to the age of 80 is no achievement at all unless it arrives with the awareness of decay, infirmity and senility. Age can be our friend or enemy; so much is conditioned by our inner response to the flowing of time. There is no use in becoming a septuagenarian or an octogenarian if you still possess a youthful mind.

To accept the idea of infirmity we must regard the age of 40 as a rebirth. You have lived your first 40 years, bought lots of CDs, been promoted, travelled a bit and compiled a list of all the people you have ever got off with. But the second half of your life will be marked by the new acceptance. It will be a literal rebirth of the old soul.

Born again old souls

The human body is a mechanism that is wearing down. Look at you. You are killing your brain cells through hangovers and still listening to heavy metal. Sometimes you muddle up your socks and put the milk in the oven instead of the fridge because you just can't cope with multi-tasking anymore. Soon you will be taking flasks of tea on day trips and worrying about the price of parking and the cost of buying refreshments at the beach and the risk of ever doing anything slightly spontaneous.

As you enter the new paradigm of sublime old age, you must stop looking at life as a fulfilling activity and instead see it as something to be endured. How few of us ever fully experience the dusty recesses and unswept bits under the skirting board of the human soul. There is a core of meaning within ourselves. You might have tolerated 40 years of youthful hedonism, but now your second life is beginning; it is time to fulfill your destiny through the acceptance of old age. Accept your limits and buy a Thermos flask. Your second birth is a time to not dance, stay immobile and be unhappy.

Do you really want to live on fruit and vegetables, rise early, take regular exercise and still be working for a stationery manufacturer for years and years so that you become a really boring 100-year-old? Thought not. Now list your true desires instead. Mine include the following:

I want to be lazy

I want to read the paper

I want to watch television

I want to drink loads

I want to remain unhealthy

I want to die doing something I'm ashamed of.

Simply through repeating these desires to yourself you have transformed the idea of old age from the threat of a lifetime of relentless yearning about how to live longer and not to succumb to any terminal diseases, to a desirable and attainable goal.

Boldly going towards oldly going

A famous study by the anthropologist Bert Bonk of the indigenous people of East Bourne revealed the psychological characteristics necessary for successful ageing. In the mysterious closed community of East Bourne a remarkably high proportion of the old souls questioned had moved in to a contentedly miserable old age. Bonk's research pinpointed the following factors as being common to successfully attaining the new old age:

- The indigenous elders of East Bourne had all learned what the sages refer to as the divine wisdom of old age. The old 'uns ignored all dietary advice, because there was always some scare about red meat, dairy products, cholesterol, saturated fat or chips inducing cancer. Instead they ate a psychologically satisfying diet of whatever they bleeding well wanted. Indeed, many put their taciturn natures down to a retirement subsisting on nothing but breakfasts of bacon, sausage, mushrooms, eggs and fried bread.

- Tribal elders ignored all lifestyle advice from doctors because if doctors were so clever, young man, then how come so many of them smoked and drank too much? They would, however, accept indefinite supplies of sleeping tablets, Valium and beta blockers.

Their bags rattled, their bedrooms looked like pharmacies. All the evidence suggests that the medicines had a valuable placebo effect, allowing them to struggle to open the childproof tops on the jars and then misread the labels and get every dosage wrong.

- They found the grey skies of a dull seaside town they forgot to close down highly conducive to melancholy ageing. Grey seascapes, soggy sand, closed ice cream parlours and candy floss sellers – these were all death-affirming props. They were deemed essential to the successfully engaging with ageing lifestyle.

- Successful long-livers all exuded a mood of pessimism. Everything was better 30 years ago, so they were certainly not going to enjoy their old age. Most subjects had successfully convinced themselves in their minds that no one at all ever locked their front door 30 years ago.

- They had irascible, highly agitated and easily annoyed personalities. Several questionnaire compilers are still recovering from stick and umbrella wounds.

- The entire sample expressed gross distrust of youth and in particular gangs of youths with hoods on hanging about car parks. Many elders advocated locking up all young people, birching them and then throwing away the key.

- They drank sherry from the late afternoon onwards. Often they would sit in saloon bars complaining about too much bureaucracy.

- They checked their building society accounts, stocks and shares regularly and were in constant fear of losing their savings. They were never content in their old age. They worried about their savings going on the cost of living in an old people's home. Many wore trousers specially designed to accommodate the traditional tribal attributes of possessing short arms and long pockets.

- They protested against all new developments or indeed any form of progress with the words 'Not in my backyard!'.

- They never walked anywhere but simply propped themselves up in bus shelters, sometimes even dying in this inert position.

- They liked chintz patterns on their crockery and a high proportion of the sample was openly proud of this fact.

Admittedly the life span of the indigenous peoples of East Bourne was shorter than that of some indigenous peoples in parts of China, Russia and Papua New Guinea where frugal lifestyles were adopted and people tilled the fields 24 hours a day without ever getting really drunk or high on natural plants. But with the advent of the new time-bound paradigm, does anyone really want to live to be 100 when your only entertainment is telling yarns to bearded anthropologists?

The people of East Bourne had achieved the ultimate state of contented curmudgeons. They were in touch with their frail old bodies' inner intelligence and had a perfect awareness of ageing. Medical drugs could never do this, nor could genetic modification or the manipulation of so-called ageing genes. The trigger for laying aside the ghost of youth and fitting on the cloak of decrepitude had come from the awareness within us all. The field sends messages and everything we do has a corresponding reaction in the field. Stars and planets collide and so too do wheelchairs and Zimmer frames.

The aged of East Bourne saw themselves as old, really old, bus-pass and end-of-the-pier-shows old. In East Bourne the concept of youth has never been accepted. All vestiges of youthful life had been discarded. They had defeated youth in a meaningful way. The struggle for new life as an old git had been won.

The benefits of avoiding exercise

A common factor in those who age successfully is undoubtedly lack of exercise. Sensible doctors will prescribe a complete lack of physical activity for all elderly folk, but unfortunately some 'progressive' GPs are now suggesting that old folk should carry on working on their muscle tone right up until the day they die.

It is important to remember that even moderate activity such as housework can cause some inadvertent aerobic activity so this is best avoided. Try not to walk up and down stairs any more than is necessary. Gardening can also burn calories and is best left to young helpers whom you can then complain at for not cutting the verges of the lawn properly. Dancing is simply a ridiculous idea for old folks who are unsteady on their feet and swimming should be shunned as a dangerous activity capable of shifting calories.

The most natural and balanced life position for the old person is to take to their armchair. Sitting in your armchair all day will allow you to forget about the tyranny of the body and concentrate on the mental powers that facilitate successful oldness. This will allow you to read newspapers and complain about political leaders and declining moral standards. It will enable you to issue instructions to home helps and long-suffering family carers and to perfect the art of annoying and irritating them with your pedantic insistence on a particular spoon with your boiled egg served in a particular egg cup, and your incredible ability to lose the remote control down the side of the armchair.

If you must exercise try to do it irregularly so it is as much a shock to the body as possible, will make you ache for days afterwards and therefore discourage you from ever trying it again.

The liberation of conscious inertia

It is typical of the cult of youth in modern society that senility and dementia is something to be feared. This sense of foreboding is symptomatic of the old paradigm. The indigenous people of East Bourne had no fears about using senility as a positive life tool. The typical symptoms of confusion, forgetfulness, disorientation, not being able to remember what year it is, or who is the Prime Minister of England or the President of the United States, provided the ideal excuse for forgetting their grandchildren's birthdays or agreeing to go out to lunch and then changing their mind for no apparent reason. Senility in the right hands can be a life-affirming gift for the old sod that wants to do just what he wants while still receiving sympathy from gullible relatives. Rudeness is excused as a symptom of extreme old age – which gives the liberated pensioner the chance to be a right old sod to younger family members.

A unique study in to ageing took place at the village of Ugley, England, in 1959. Subjects from the ages of 20 to 100 were tested to see how their organs atrophied over time. The Longitudinal Study of Ugley People, to give it its full title, produced a wealth of data. Key conclusions supported the theory of new oldness and old newness in the new paradigm. These included:

When people age the effects can vary hugely. Some unfortunate subjects are still trying to build up their muscles at the age of 80; other more aware individuals simply concentrate on muscle wastage and inertia.

Alcohol has a much quicker effect on old people than on young people. Moderation and abstemiousness is wasted on the elderly. Most older people greatly enjoyed being able to get drunk on a couple of half pints of lager shandy.

Remaining sexually active in old age is not a good idea. Those Viagra bills are high and no one wants to hear a pair of pensioners going at it in the next hotel room. Many subjects found the thought of love bites on chicken necks repulsive.

The most contented senior citizens were those who could talk about the war for hours to youngsters who were not at all interested.

Many old people show a remarkable increase in verbal dexterity when given the chance to accost and bore a younger subject who has a pressing appointment and is desperately trying to edge their way towards the door.

Surliness, irrationality and irritability can only be maintained through constant practising. If you do not use your grumpiness faculties, they may atrophy and you risk slipping into a state of aged amiability. Grumpiness is the highest spiritual state attained by the old masters and we must always aim towards it on our journey to conscious inertia and sublime surliness. Impaired mental facilities can only be attained through years of transcendental wittering and some subtle feigning of symptoms to the youngsters.

Our bodies are being reshaped at the quantum level throughout our lives. Bonk's evidence is only a small part of what we have so far discovered about new oldness in the bold new paradigm. But to truly be aware of our oldness there is one subject that must be reassessed: the sex lives of the elderly.

The myth of perpetual sexuality

One of the biggest deceivers of the perpetually young is the myth of an active sex life for old people. In previous generations old people were in touch with their natural bio-rhythms; they knew that sex was not for them when there were more suitable activities such as knitting, bowls and dominos. Yet today, a generation still wearing jeans is seeking what they term self-expression. They separate after their children have grown up and seek sexual fulfillment, which they feel has been denied them. They get new haircuts and leather jackets and join dating agencies for pensioners. Some 64-year-olds even realign their sexuality and discover that they are gay or lesbian and enter same-sex relationships. When they do this they appear to have no consideration for their children. It's bad enough to know your parents are having sex at all, let alone changing their sexuality.

When I have clients asking for Viagra I know that the problem is not that are lacking virility; what they are really lacking is knowledge of their own decrepitude. An active sex life with frequent orgasms and the onrush of ageing pheromones is very dangerous for the senior citizen. It can lead to euphoria, enhanced positive mood swings and even regeneration at the cellular level. We can only really attain exemplary old age when we acknowledge that sex is not for the likes of us oldies.

Knowing that sex is an activity done by young people allows the sexless septuagenarian to nurture feelings of jealousy and envy, which in turn help foster the state of irritability and tone of disapproval adopted by successful elders. Living with someone you no longer sleep with is perfect for nurturing feelings of irascibility and mood swings that will successfully antagonise younger people. Empty hedonism can never replace the inner truth of perfect unity with the ageing process.

To counter this fashion we must cultivate and work at the concept of a sexless life. If you need help with this concept, see the helpful pointers on the next pages.

20 STEPS TOWARDS NOT HAVING SEX

1. Consider your bad back. Listen to the cellular intelligence revealing that its muscles are in spasm. Is it really up to all that humping and pumping?

2. Remember that no one of your age wants to sleep on a damp patch.

3. Consider the indignity of boasting to your children about your latest one-night stand.

4. Remind yourself of the sniggering in the chemist when you last purchased some extra-safe condoms.

5. Subscribe to a good sports channel so there is always a big match on to take your mind off carnal thoughts.

6. If you are tempted to have sex with another old person then turn the light on so that you can see all their bodily imperfections first.

7. Try not to remember your lover as he or she was 30 or 40 years ago. Memories of the past can delude us all. Look at your lover with an objective eye; see them for the person they are today. They are not 20 anymore. They have turned in to an old person with cellulite and bi-focals and flabby bits. Concentrate on one bodily imperfection, focus on it, concentrate, and carry on doing this until the remnants of desire are gone forever.

8. Try to imagine that all your extended family are watching you in the sack and laughing at you.

9. Think dentures rather than Durex.

10. Take up bingo instead.

11. Focus on all the negative things that your partner has ever said to you, be it comments on your snoring/washing up/innate sexism/perpetual PMT/inability to leave the loo seat down. Concentrate on all that bitterness and then try to perceive that person in a sexual manner.

12. Accept the gift of ugliness. You are wrinkled, saggy and unloveable. There are warts on your face. You have nothing to prove any more.

13. Place a particularly interesting biography by your bed so that you always have a distraction from unwanted carnal thoughts.

14. Invite your children to come and live with you, pointing out that as property prices are so high they might as well stay in the room next door to yours.

15. Never wash your private parts or underwear.

16. Never give gifts or unsolicited compliments. Cultivate an inner sense of irascibility instead.

17. Consider the fate of John Entwistle, the late bass player in the Who, who had a heart attack at the age of 57, after taking cocaine and a night of debauchery in a hotel room with a Las Vegas stripper.

18. Get into God.

19. Sniff your socks when you take them off, then announce they should be good for another few days' wear.

20. Burp, dribble or pass wind at important moments of foreplay.

Attaining meaningful oldness

Let us forget all talk of sex and fulfillment and even worse, personal growth. The human mind is full of infinite possibilities; we can age as much as we want to. To be old is to be nearly dead and to joyously accept the fact. Soon the time of baby boomers with backpacks and motorbikes will be gone. We are moving towards a grey new world, where adrenaline rushes for wrinklies are banished and surliness and inertia are positively celebrated. In the field of intention we are moving towards blissful and meaningful oldness.

You can choose the life you want. We can unite mind, body and spirits. The highest form of freedom is total mastery of your objectives within the wholeness of existence. Below I have listed my ten steps towards inactive mastery:

1. Burn incense, wear crystals around your neck, go to Glastonbury Tor, hug standing stones and trees, hear the inner music of the cosmos, listen to your body and then ignore it.

2. Live in the past. Back then everything was as it should be and all without video recorders, mobile phones, DVDs, CD-Roms and laptops. And iPods, whatever they are. We didn't need chatrooms, oh no, back then we made our own entertainment.

3. Noisiness is inner strength. Take time to be noisy. Set aside an hour everyday for shouting at the mirror and punching inanimate objects. Shout from the window, go to the attic and shout from the roof. Shout at people in the street. Rage at the world.

4. Only do what others approve of. There's nothing old people like more than obeying rules and shopping people who are illegally parked. Phone the council regularly, pester town planning and parking officials and the recycling officer. Memorise obscure by-laws. Make it your responsibility to see that the law is enforced however much it annoys your neighbours.

5. Nurture your anger. When you find yourself wanting to hit someone in queues at the bank or at the bus stop, follow your intuition. This is the essence of inner freedom. The fist is your friend. The physical and the mental are inseparable at the quantum level. Be aware of your innate capacity for holistic violence and nurture it.

6. Move towards absolute self-awareness. Look into the mirror and see the old person staring back at you. Forget all thoughts of emotional projection – old gits like you never get parts in the movies. Have the courage to be what you are – an old fossil.

7. Judge everyone, especially those who have recently infuriated you. Encourage your innate anger and demand stiffer penalties and less understanding for all perpetrators of crime. Demand that they bring back hanging for everyone. Tell people on the bus about your views.

8. Contaminate your body with as many toxins as you can. Alcohol, caffeine, cigarette smoke, medicines in jars with screw-tops you can never get undone – all are excellent facilitators of

unpredictable and irrational responses. Only when you have reached toxin overload will you reach the spiritual state of heightened rage necessary for the nirvana of irascible old age.

9. Nurture past hurts. Remember them, dwell on them, brood on them. Bear grudges. Lots of them. Especially against that bully who hit you when you were 11. Be motivated by fear and envy. Tread heavily on people's dreams.

10. Remember that the world is just a great big onion and that's why it's making you cry so much. The planet is organic, hence it is going mouldy just like the vegetables at the top of your compost bin. So is the quantum universe. We are all part of a higher disunity leading to perfect tetchiness and addictions to tearooms. The greatest good is the impure life. Only soon you'll be dead anyway, so you won't have to worry about this mystical stuff at all.

In practice: Balancing your korma

Inactive mastery is not easily obtained. It involves an immersion in life, an absolute devotion to the demands of the mind-body duality. Many of the Indian sages have achieved the wisdom that comes with old age, pot bellies and grey hair, while some even get to hang out with pop groups. They have all paid attention to attaining spiritual balance through diet. The life force that flows through every pore of their bodies is known as korma. Several food sources can nurture korma, be it in chicken, lamb, prawn or vegetables.

When korma is balanced the mind may experience sudden moments of alertness and insight, particularly when aided by lager libations, before the sage slumps head first into his rice, exhausted from the ecstasy of pure korma energy buzzing through his body. When korma is perfected the subject can sometimes feel a rush of energy, sweat poring from the brow and a pulsing in the bowel. This is often passed off as a desire to rush to the loo, but this is only the way society has taught us to perceive our bodily insights.

The ancient wisdom teaches us that the source of korma can be found on the breath, which as the old sages say, is the spaghetti junction of the mind-body duality. The quality of your korma is reflected in your breathing. Slow inhaling and taking time to sense the delicate aromas of korma will ensure a state of balance in your body.

Flowing korma encourages alertness, enthusiasm, a pleasing sense of reduced motor coordination, sensations of thirst and moments of blissful spiritual awareness, when you attain the mental clarity necessary to both run the country and pick a football team. It stimulates the body's levels of additives, food dyes and hot spices. Enhanced korma will precipitate a tingle within your internal organs at an organic level. The individual with balanced korma will feel alert and at one with his or her bodily functions. All followed by a ritual purging of impurities and toxins from the human digestive system. Every breath should enhance your korma and lead you away from false ideals of fitness towards a unifying spiritual and physical flabbiness.

EXERCISE 1: Toxic breath

Find a noisy place where you can sit still. On the verge of a busy motorway junction would be just about perfect. Listen to the roar of the juggernauts, the pounding of car stereos turned up to maximum volume, the piercing wail of ambulance and traffic police sirens, the horns blaring at traffic lights when someone stalls, the drivers shouting obscenities at one another. Observe the one-finger salutes and the waving fists.

Fix your eyes on a plastic cone and concentrate on your breath. Feel the wheezing sensation build up in your chest, be aware of the dirt and exhaust fumes wafting upwards through your nostrils. Feel the exterior toxins integrating with your body. Be aware that you are now moving towards harmony with your cacophonous and ugly environment. Concentrate on your breath until you feel the asthmatic wheeze of an old person pulsing through your body. Don't stop until you sound like Dennis Hopper in *Blue Velvet*.

EXERCISE 2: Encouraging the red mist of anger

While wearing nothing but your worst Argyle socks, stand in the room of the house that annoys you the most. Focus on a moment from the past where you felt terribly hurt and really really angry. Try to recapture that feeling of exasperation, desperation and depression. It might be that bastard who fired you, the person who was unfaithful or dumped you for no reason, or the striker who missed an open goal in the last minute of an important football match. Or it could be that time the train broke down in the middle of the Scottish Highlands in the early hours during a blizzard, or the terrible accident with a Hoover suction pipe that did it for your Uncle Albert. It could be the time you walked in on the ex-love of your life having torrid and passionate sex with your former best friend.

Wave your fist at God and curse Him for forcing existence upon you. Move your arms up and down in a rhythmic dance of hate. Close your eyes and you will be aware of darting red orbs of lights and then a pulsing light throbbing through your consciousness. Let that red light expand through your body. Take short, sharp, angry breaths. Let the red mist course out of you with every agitated, fretful breath.

This is a very unpleasant exercise that will successfully enable you to enhance your biological age. It will leave your body tingling with repressed anger and fear, aggravate existing skin conditions and ultimately leave you at one with the bad feelings penetrating every orifice of your body.

Twenty signs of successful anger management

1. Reddened cheeks

2. High blood pressure

3. Stick waving or fist shaking

4. Unbuttoned cardigans

5. Abusive references to the youth of today

6. Swearing

7. Puncturing of kids' footballs

8. Wielding of garden secateurs

9. Phone calls to the police

10. Cardiac arrests

11. Spluttering

12. Brandishing of Strimmer

13. Pointing

14. Fist shaking

16. Public urination over possessions of those who have offended you

17. Smashing of car windows

18. Brandishing of baseball bat

19. Threats to neighbours' pets

20. Removal of family from your last Will and testament.

CHAPTER 5
BREAKING THE MOULD
OF YOUTH

In the conventional world – the so-called real world that we inhabit – no one appears to worry about ageing. Middle-aged people have embarrassing office affairs, grandmothers go rock climbing, fly in hot air balloons and test-drive Ferraris. Pensioners talk openly about seeking adrenaline rushes. Instead of staying with their life partner and living lives of morose tedium – an ideal background for becoming an old git – grey panthers are spouting stuff about personal fulfillment, divorcing and joining dating agencies. Some are even speed dating.

The baby boomers that grew up in the post-war population boom, who became student rebels in the 1960s and pioneered social change, are refusing to age with dignity. They are outnumbering young people and reject the fact that they are no longer young.

A grey new world
At an exterior level this world of people who refuse to age appears to be normal. It is easy to follow others on the path to jogging while listening to iPods. It is not so easy to perceive of a different world

view, to hear the eternal truth of oldness in the air, the atmosphere, the outer regions of quantum space.

Yet there is another world; another land where time's drum is beating ever faster and you are marching relentlessly towards the place where the human spirit is enveloped in grey anoraks, where reading glasses, paisley pyjamas and hatred of change are propelling you towards joyous oblivion.

Occasionally during visionary moments we can glimpse this second world. It is a time-bound place where hairs are turning grey as we look at them, muscles are wasting and motor functions are winding down. The dramatic scientists Withnail and Marwood, both eminent professors at the Camden Institute, described this place perfectly. Observing an over-medicated client called Daniel, Marwood opined, 'His mechanism's gone!'.

We only see this second world rarely, in moments of heightened consciousness and spiritual fulfillment. This is a kind of epiphany of your old soul where, for a brief moment, we sense the disunity of all things, we become aware of the Divine scheme that is encouraging us all to age, wither and die. We have all experienced such moments during our lives when worldly appearances are shown to be false and we see things as they really are. Because they do not fit in easily with scientific theories they have been classified as religious experiences, whereas in scientific terms you are in fact catching a glimpse of the true nature of the quantum field. It is old and it is dying. You are caught in time-bound reality.

Once the spirit of mortality is infused within every aspect of your being, every breath you take, then you can experience ageing right here, right now, in this decrepit old body you haul around every day. This is the time-bound experience that the new paradigm of sublime oldness has been preparing us for.

Accepting linear time

Time is your enemy. Einstein might have discovered that time was relative, but then he went and died which rather ruined his theory. In the quantum field, time can move backwards, forwards, sideways and quite possibly breakdance. But that's not much use to you now, is it? Even physicists striving for a unified theory of everything get old and die. We can make time do all sorts of things on blackboards and Open University programmes, but it still won't stop your paunch from sagging over the top of your belt.

A dead parrot cannot move backwards in time. The certainty of death was expressed with great clarity by *Monty Python's Flying Circus*, when the metaphysical genius that is John Cleese declared with sublime insight: 'This parrot is no more. He has ceased to be… He's snuffed it!'.

It is no coincidence that book editors are obsessed with deadlines. They have no concept of timelessness and are blessed by an innate intelligence sending information to their bodies at the cellular level, urging them to adhere to a time-bound life. In our modern youth-obsessed society they have somehow retained the innate wisdom of the 'just effing well get on with it' school of time-bound philosophy.

Deadlines hold a mirror up to life. If you don't hand in your manuscript on time then your lines really are dead. Tardy writers get nowhere except the slush pile. The time-bound publisher will get someone else to write the thing or postpone your book's launch date for another five years. If you die before you hand in the manuscript then that really messes up the publication schedule. Those who can't embrace deadlines are losers in the lottery of the time-bound cosmos. We must learn to accept, and even love, deadlines. Be pressured by time, be worried by it. Admit you're getting old and that soon your personal deadline will be reached.

Our life span is governed by linear time. That's why you need Viagra, you silly old sod. No one is getting any younger. This can be expressed in the fairly complex evolutionary formula below. Do not worry if at first you do not understand this. Allow awareness to flow through your body, study the significance of the life stages listed below and you will slowly accept the inevitable truth of onrushing linear time.

Birth
Childhood
Adolescence
Youth
Middle age
Old gitdom
DEATH

The way we age depends on how our body responds to time. Those who do not feel threatened by time are at risk of never ageing. Imagine what a terrible life that must be, trapped forever in the world of Wilde's *Dorian Gray*, yearning to escape the tyranny of personal trainers and dating people 20 years younger than yourself. Only those who see time as a threat will ever experience the full joy of feeling miserably old. As I have explained previously, stress can be the great liberator of the timeless. The more stress you can store in your body through worrying about deadlines the better. Those who are successfully time-bound will:

- Feel that if someone is one minute late for a lift then it is perfectly acceptable to drive off without their passenger

- Always feel pressured by deadlines

- Always feel that there are not enough hours in the day to facilitate all the moaning they want to do

- Set several alarm clocks every morning

- Shop only on busy Saturdays and make sure they block the supermarket aisle with that huge trolley that they still haven't learned to manoeuvre properly

- Carry several bus and train timetables in their pockets

- Get on the bus and argue with the driver about why his bus is seven minutes later than the time specified on the timetable

- Carry voluminous road atlases and when arriving at their children's houses spend an inordinate amount of time discussing routes

- Never have read a new age book in their life

- Never embraced the spiritual side of their nature or burnt joss sticks

- Never have time to think about God.

When the time-bound nature is embraced then the real self can open itself to the pure force of oldness. Have you ever noticed the similarities between the words old and God? Both have three letters and they both contain the letters 'o' and 'd', so there must be something in this.

Once the time-bound essence within us is discovered a seismic shock takes place in our awareness. Skateboards and knee pads are consigned to the cellar. Lycra cycling shorts become repellent as you picture wobbling flesh drooping over a straining saddle. Rock climbing shoes are thrown from the nearest sea cliff as you realise the joys of vertigo. Motorbikes are traded in for motorized wheelchairs as you discover that the ultimate rush of joy comes not from speed but from delay.

We are all on a journey of linear time from A to B. Athletics is for school children, not grown adults. The Olympics are for the young;

you feel tired just watching them on television with a beer in your hand. This is all part of the disjointed quantum field theory which can be expressed as:

Quantum field → Track and field → Playing field

The quantum universe has a beginning and an end. The theory of everything will never be found. Accept this truth. Accept reality and let it pulse through your being. Cease your false striving and learn to love your saggy body with its sacks of decaying muscle and fat and gristle for what it is. If only we can transcend our fear of youth then we can redefine forever our place in the universe.

Overcoming the illusion of youth

Just to assume that there is a concept called youth is a half-truth. Youth is only delayed ageing; follicles are already decaying, the cells that programme our white hairs are already in evidence, your skin is being burnt by solar rays and wrinkles are waiting to emerge. No amount of carbonated mineral water, Walkmans, jogging shoes and MTV piped in to the gym will ever change this fact. You are like particularly mature Brie that has been in the fridge of life for far too long.

Yet ultimately we are not suffering fear of youth but ignorance of youth. We think of youth as something pleasurable yet we forget the misery and the mental strain of exuding constant exuberance and ebullience. Youth is to be despised not treasured.

The cycle of life is a constant round of change moving ever onwards towards death and disaster. Yet our life programming is sadly inadequate. So many of my patients are unable to cope with the inevitability of slip-on shoes and egg stains on their shirts, instead longing for the false contentment of a happy and contented sexual and personal life way into their 80s.

Think back to your childhood and the positive images of youth that were forced upon you by your parents. Their intentions might have been good, but throughout your childhood they were inadvertently reinforcing the social stereotypes of youth being a desirable goal. Where were the positive images of not bothering with shopping at Gap and instead wearing jumpers from charity shops? When you were a six-year-old, did mum and dad ever tell you about the life-affirming joy to be had from moaning, whingeing, hating youngsters and generally being a reactionary git?

Forget all thoughts of immortality. When you die your body will decompose and all that grave mulch will go towards fertilizing trees, but that's not much compensation to you now, is it? OK, your DNA will be passed on to your kids, if you have any, but we all know that that DNA is wasted upon the young.

No, we are time-bound and as the mechanism that is our body is running down the ultimate liberation comes only through acceptance of this fact. Your life is flowing towards the ultimate attainment of geriatric grace. Oldness is permanent, deep and forever.

You can claim the ultimate prize of being at one with your old self. The song of the senile is with us always. Cast your jogging shoes away on to the landfill site full of false promises of youth. Accept the awesome truth of bladder weakness. Rejoice in breasts heading south. Bumbling old fools are breathing on the winds of eternity. Feel the irregular beat of your heart. Concentrate on the pleasure of your raised blood pressure. Listen to the music contained within the words I AM OLD. I AM AN OLD CODGER. I AM A SILLY OLD FOOL.

In practice:
EXERCISE 1
The deepest awareness of decrepitude gives you inner power. The ancient sages knew this eternal truth. As long as your life is governed by the principles of decay and destruction then you can continue to grow old. When you are sitting in the field of oldness you can experience the full flow of onrushing dementia. Enjoy the accolades of being described as cantankerous, misanthropic, grumpy, bossy, irascible, curmudgeonly, churlish, haggish, witch-like, wizened and dried-up. Above all make a commitment to these seven qualities:

1. **Experience noise**
   Our old souls can only be nourished in a cacophonous environment. Allocate some time every day to experiencing noise. Poke sticks at the rotweiller in the neighbour's garden. Stand next to workmen wielding pneumatic drills or cars at traffic lights with their windows down and the stereo playing techno or garage at full volume. Swear at young men wearing hooded jackets. Bump in to young men wearing bling jewellery. Shout at policemen. Abuse

drunks and attempt to steal their super-strength lager. All these activities should generate a pleasing amount of decibels. Noise is a valuable commodity. Too often we are lulled in to peace and silence or even worse, meditation. Grumpiness and irascibility are nurtured through noise.

2. Spend time in cities

Your body is at one with the cycles of the city; milkmen arriving, dustmen hoisting black bags from rubbish bins, noisy former lovers shouting abuse at each other and threatening violence, gangs of youths smashing up telephone boxes, steaming gangs on the trains, police sirens throughout the night, police helicopters whirring up above in the sky, burglars breaking through your skylight. In the countryside there is nothing to complain about. Nature is nice but boring. It is only in the unfettered and untamed urban environment that the sage old person can complain with impunity. The naked flame of anger can burn as brightly as a really well constructed bonfire lit by homeless people on a piece of urban waste ground. The city is the only home for the old at heart.

3. Distrust all your emotions

Emotional literacy is for those who believe in the fallacy of perpetual youth. Be on the lookout for liberal emotions and then suppress them ruthlessly. Old people have no time for love or compassion. Liberate yourself through the flow of misanthropy, which permeates all conscious thought. Compile a journal in which you note down all your negative feelings. Work on one example each day and then try to recreate it through the power of negative thought. Take that piece of paper full of negative emotions with you wherever you go. Give attention and nurturing to your anger and hurt and feelings of insecurity in a world perpetually changing for the worse. Read your list and remind yourself that these feelings can grow organically to take over your entire life.

4. Remain chaotic in the midst of calm

It is not easy to remain chaotic when all around you are calm. It takes specific skills and attributes to cultivate chaos. Move to the untidiest room in the house. Concentrate on your breathing. Try to hyperventilate. Remember past panic-attacks and try to recreate that feeling again. Breathe into a paper bag if that helps get back the sensation of short breath and onrushing hysteria.

Concentrate on raising your pulse and blood pressure. Stimulate any nervous twitches with caffeine, alcohol or mind-expanding concoctions. Then scatter papers around the room. Throw away your diaries and clocks. Never keep appointments. Never throw anything away. Don't wash up. Take all your books off the bookshelf and instead place them in teetering piles around the house. Hide your phone. Don't answer emails. Deliberately set the video clock to the wrong time and then leave it flashing away in an irritating manner.

Do not resist chaos. You will slowly discover that being chaotic and irrational is actually your natural state. The old person you really are lives in a state of mayhem, doubt and vacillation, nurtured by uncreative chaos.

5. Hate all children

Children are the enemy of the old. Never play games with them, never be childlike. Instead confiscate their balls when they land in your garden and refuse to contribute to their school fund or buy their raffle tickets.

Children are infected with optimism and enthusiasm. They believe in good causes and world peace. They refuse to embrace disillusion and disgrace. They follow fashion. They have sex lives to look forward to. They try to bring food round to old people. They'll never have to work as hard as you did. Their parents indulge them and buy them far too many presents. Write down everything you hate about children. Then resolve to be horrible to one of them right now.

If you really must be with children then try to reassure yourself that with climate change, all that buried nuclear waste, coming water scarcity, the likelihood of an asteroid striking Earth and the cloning of human embryos, they really don't have much to be optimistic about at all.

6. Be selfish

To attain the highest stage of oldness the aged person must be truly selfish. Total absorption in the self is the sign of the rigid and disciplined old git. Once we lose the trappings of selflessness then we can be who we really are. Old people don't care about social justice or the world around them. Their world view is narrow, blinkered and irrational. Let us strip away the veneer of concern for others and enjoy concern only about ourselves. Altruism is the province of the young. In the land where everyone is old, the self is centre of all our lives. Life is about me, me, me. Be grasping, be avaricious and be mendacious. Let feelings of darkness envelop your body; allow the true selfish old sod that is you to come out in to the light.

7. **Become attached to absurd routines**
   Surround yourself with clutter and emotional baggage. Be absolutely rigid in your routine. Insist to your children that you must always go shopping on a Wednesday because that's the day you do it and that's final whether they want to visit you or not. Never opt for new experiences. Who wants breakdancing septuagenarians? Chasing new adrenaline highs is dangerous and wild and not for old folks like you. Don't write your life experiences down or attempt to analyse past experiences. Remember that things were always better in the past. Self-knowledge is for the timeless not the time-bound. Cultivate your inner reactionary. Moan about everything. Don't eat your food. Rejoice in being a bed blocker at your local hospital.

Hating yourself versus hating the world

Getting old is a pain in the posterior so why shouldn't you make everyone else suffer as well? After all, that's the only enjoyment you can get now. As the ancient aphorism goes: 'Life's a bitch and then you die'. Whoever composed that line had a profound sense of what true wisdom and knowledge are. Our lives are flowing towards the place where everyone has a bus pass but the buses are always late.

In the land beyond change there is short change and you have undoubtedly been short-changed in the fiasco of your life. The more you can experience hate and bitterness the more you are moving towards your elderly essence.

You have permission to hate. Hate kids, Hate change. Hate the world. Think about hate and all its profound implications. Seek out hate and misery. Your body can respond to hate at a deep inner level. When hate courses through your body you are at one with the silly old fool who created life and the Universe as some form of bad joke. When you are cleansed of the spiritual and the altruistic emotions that infect our lives you can experience true life as a miserable old git. Only the enlightened old man or woman can say with clarity and insight 'I am hateful. I am never happy. It's only being so miserable and annoying you lot so much that keeps me going. I'd die right now if it wasn't too much trouble'.

All hate and negative feelings come from within. We all have the power to step into the realm of timeless irascibility. Make it your duty to encourage reactionary old sods and hold up the thrusting energy of youth. Real hate gains satisfaction from flowing through the varicose veins of the terminally grumpy. Use bitterness as your mirror to the time-bound world of the present. Unleash the power of the cardigan.

CONCLUSION

The world is changing and the time of the new old paradigm has arrived. There are numerous paths to being truly old, but surliness is the surest. Humans need no longer be victims of youth. Hopefully this book will have given the reader the tools and strategies to create an extraordinary transformation into old age. We have come on a long and extraordinary journey together.

Many of the practical exercises in this book will have given the reader an insight into the mystical unifying force of creation that is encouraging us to be aware of our own mortality. Or at least they will have given you an excuse to sit on a mat in your back garden, which is better than going to the gym. The gift of oldness is available to us all if only we have the awareness to accept it. When you started reading this book you might have felt quite youthful; it is my earnest hope that by now you are feeling truly old.

We are all cast adrift upon the wind of change. For too long western civilisation has been based upon a lie. Look at the symptoms of the modern disease all around us: people who are old but acting like they are 25. The tyranny of the toupee and the trophy wife has taken over show business and now it threatens us all.

Yet there is beauty in oblivion. We must learn to accept the gift of ugliness, the thrill of tired muscles, creaking bones and the death-affirming tingle of arthritic pain. Oldness reaches out to those who speak its name. It flows through the heart of the person who puts aside the veil of youth. If God did not intend us to grow old He would not have invented osteopaths.

One person accepting they are old is but a handful of brackish water in a slimy village pond, but if you encourage decrepitude and infirmity then it can grow to become the pond itself.

Use age as your looking glass. Let it nourish your knowledge that you are not beyond oldness; you are sprouting nasal hair as you read these words. There are numerous methods of discovering the true path to successful ageing, but time shines the brightest light. We are all trapped in the vortex of time; it is a maelstrom of change that is dragging us towards blissful senility.

It is your duty to tell those around you that they are getting old. Spread the word, tell them they are grey, knackered and past it, regardless of what you may receive in return. Let our time-bound destiny unite us.

Through the power of the mind allied to our new knowledge of the quantum field, we can increase our awareness of our cosmic destiny. We are all getting older by the day and there is sod all we can do about it. Reject the self-perpetuating and futile cycle of virtuous youth. The time has arrived to enter the sublime world of the ageing body and confused mind.

Also by Pete May:

The Lad Done Bad

Sunday Muddy Sunday: The Heart and Soul
of Sunday League Football

West Ham: Irons in the Soul

Football and Its Followers

Rent Boy: How One Man Spent 20 Years
Falling Off the Property Ladder